Life
as we know it

A Collection of Poetry

ELAINE GIBBONS

Copyright © 2022 by Elaine Gibbons

Paperback: 978-1-7374272-5-4
eBook: 978-1-7374272-4-7
Library of Congress Control Number: 2022903530

All rights reserved. No part of this publication may be reproduced, distributed, or transmitted in any form or by any electronic or mechanical means, without the prior written permission of the publisher, except in the case of brief quotations embodied in critical reviews and certain other noncommercial uses permitted by copyright law.

This is a work of nonfiction.

SWEETSPIRE LITERATURE
———— MANAGEMENT ————

ACKNOWLEDGEMENT

I acknowledge my debt to God, and thank him for this wonderful gift of expression.

SPECIAL THANKS

To my sister Kathy, Rae and dear friends Bentley and Paul, who have always supported me and been a constant source of encouragement and inspiration. David Skins, thanks for helping me to get to another level. To all who have read and bought my books, thank you very much, you have been a blessing.

DEDICATION

I dedicate this book to the youth of today, who are trying to stay alive, survive, love and live in peace

"I've learned that people will forget what you said, people will forget what you did, but people will never forget how you made them feel"

By Mayo Angelou

TABLE OF CONTENTS

CHAPTER 1 — BE POSITIVE..1

How we live 3

Be encouraged..5

Change 7

Educate them 8

I know who i am 10

Dream, believe and achieve..11

2016 And me 13

I made it out 15

I made the right choice 17

Be thankful..19

Hope for 2022...20

How to be confident...22

How to be happy 23

I hope 24

What is hope?...26

You inspire me 27

Yes you can 28

CHAPTER 2 — LIFE 29

The waiting room..31

What a shame 33

Children...35

Unexplained feelings..37

Traffic...39

He got it wrong 41
Loneliness 43
What makes me happy 45
Where's my boyfriend? 46
Our community 47
Lord i'm tired 49
Nature 52
Haters 53
Forgive them 54
He was depressed 55
Watch your mouth 57
Who am i? 58

CHAPTER 3 — LOVE 59
What is it? 61
My mom 62
I love her 63
When you love someone 64
My valentine 66
My father 67
My love and i 68
She's blessed 69
A father and son 70
My one and only 71
Just let me 72
What you mean to me 73
What i really think 74
To love, you and me 75
She loves him 76

CHAPTER 4 — MY GOD 79

There's no one like him 81
The one 83
Why i pray 84
Dear lord 85
How good is god? 86
Please god 87

CHAPTER 5 — REALITY 89

Crimes against humanity 91
Life on lockdown 94
Life 96
My view on lockdown 97
Men 99
She ain't happy 101
No identity 103
A girls story 105
A boys story 107
The system 110
They kill 112
He changed 114
Whats up fam? 116
Don't' do it 117
New kids on the block 119
You can say no 122
Black male 124
Backlash 125
These days 127
De pickney dem 130

Women	132
Remember when	134
Me dear chile	136
Some black history	138
The youth of today 2019	141
This was her reality	144

CHAPTER ONE
BE POSITIVE

"If you get, give. If you learn, teach"
"Success is liking yourself, liking what you do,
and liking how you do it"
"Success is loving life and daring to live it"

By Mayo Angelou

ELAINE GIBBONS

HOW WE LIVE

There's no manual to life
You just have to do your best
There will be trials and tribulations
And you will be put to the test.
Do well onto others
It will be a blessing onto you
Be positive in your thoughts
And let your actions follow thru
Take responsibility for your actions
And learn to say sorry when you're wrong
You need to be forgiving
Don't keep bad feelings for too long
In life you need to show love
You need to try and live in peace
Life's too short to stay angry
So all your fears you must release
You need good principles and values
And you need to speak the truth
You need to be a good example
To the up and coming youth
You need to believe in yourself
And make your dreams come true
You need to know that you can make it
No matter what others say about you
Stay connected to positive people
And let the negative ones go
If people mean you no good

Their true colours will often show
There's no manual to life
But be confident, be faithful, stand strong
Always try and do the right thing
And be thankful when better comes along.

© 2014

BE ENCOURAGED

We all have gifts and talents
We all have something to give
We're on this earth for a purpose
And it's for more than just to live
We need to make today count
Because of tomorrow we do not know
We need to do the best we can
We will only reap the seeds we sow.
We need to work hard
And be good to others
We need to have a good heart
Towards our sisters and brothers
We need to be positive
In all the things we do
We need to be a blessing
And an encouragement too
We are to show manners and respect to others
We are to grow our youth the right way
We need to lead by good example
As they are the future of today.
We are to be truthful to ourselves and others
We are to accept when we are wrong
We need to know we can achieve
We need to believe that we are strong.
We need to learn how to be patient
And not to rush into everything
Not all that glitters is gold

And unhappiness it may bring
Life has its ups and downs
Its pleasures and its pain
But life is what you make it
And what you put in is what you gain.

© 2015

CHANGE

Change is always happening
And seasons's come and go
Some change is natural and can't be stopped
It can give us time to grow
A baby is born
While our loved one's die
This change is a must
There's no point to asking why
New friendships will blossom
And old one's drift away
Seize the day and enjoy it
You need to focus on today
Change is an opportunity
For us to change too
For us to become better people
But change has to start with you
It must begin with something positive
And you have to change your mind
Embrace it, make it work for you
And it will all work out in time.

© 2014

EDUCATE THEM

Education is the key
For the youth of today
It needs to start real early
So they don't fall along the way

For some it's just a cycle
Of violence, poverty and crime
They grow up believing nothing else
We need to catch those ones in time

Before they go out into the world
And before they grow up street
It needs to start at Junior School
Because who knows who they might meet

We know it should start with parents
But some are too busy to care
Some really ain't got a clue
But for a child, that's just not fair

We all have a responsibility
The community should grow that child
Safeguard with discipline and boundaries
Manners and respect should be applied

Education is the key
But life on the street is real
The curriculum's of the utmost importance
But Guns and Gangs are now a big deal

I know it won't be apart of every child's life
But they still just need to know
To say No to knives, Guns and Crime
But if they get caught up, there's a place to go

They need a place of safety
They need a friendly face
They need not to be judged
Or regarded as a disgrace

The youth of today are in trouble
Their looting, shooting, some die
We need to educate our youth
So no more parents have to cry.

© 2015

ELAINE GIBBONS

I KNOW WHO I AM

I want to be better than I am
I want to be more, and I can
I want those letters after my name
I want to be different, so that's my claim.
I want to be remembered
For something great
I want to make people smile
And I know it's not too late.
I want to stay creative
And be positive too
I want to leave a legacy
For all of you.
I want to help the community
I want to show that I care
I want to do something special
So challenge me if you dare.
To use my skills, knowledge and experience
And to gain new ones today
I don't just want to be like everyone else
I want to try and pave the way.
For others to know their purpose
For those who dream to achieve
For those who hope and move forward
I'll make a difference, in this I believe.

Inspired by Pastor Raymond Williams and Bentley Noble

© 8th Nov 2015

DREAM, BELIEVE AND ACHIEVE

You're a kid at school
Or a student at college
You're a graduate at uni
And your heads full of all this knowledge
Some say knowledge is the key
But which doors will it open
Will it give you what you need?
That depends on which road you've chosen.
Life's full of opportunities
We all need to have a dream
We need to have something to hope for
And not focus on what could have been.
As a kid I want to be this
As a student I'm working towards that
I'm an adult now and I've made it
So it's time to look forward not back.
We all have the ability to achieve
And we can make our dreams come true
Opportunity gives us the tools to do it
Just decide what's important to you.
I suppose what I'm trying to say is
You need ambition to succeed
Don't scream and shout when one door closes
Lift yourself up and take the lead.
This is about believing in you
It's about using your talent
It's about using your gift
And not letting it go stagnant.

If you don't try, then you won't know
How great you could have been
Time definitely waits for no one
But faith is hoping for things unseen.
So take a leap of faith
And go for what you want
I believe that you can achieve it
So don't let anyone say you can't.

© 2015

2016 AND ME

New Year, New start
It's two thousand and sixteen
I'm all geared up and focused
So let me tell you what I mean.
It's a chance to forget the past
It's a chance to start something new
New goals and ambitions
It's not about others point of view.
I won't give up if it's a struggle
And won't give up if some say so
Perseverance is what I'll roll with
Because endurance is what I know.
It's about how I'm going to progress in life
It's about how I'm gonna succeed
Positive thoughts, a good mind and heart
These are just some of the things I'll need.
But life is for living
So I'll take a risk or two
And I'll strive to better myself
In everything I do.
This year may have its ups and downs
But through it I will stand strong
I'll work hard and stay focused
Because that's been my plan all along.
I won't focus on how others live
Who knows what goes on behind closed doors
I'll never grudge what another man has
And I won't rebel without a cause.

This year I'll do the best I can
And bless everyday with a smile
So do good and it will follow you
Because were only here but for a while.

© 2nd Jan 2016

I MADE IT OUT

Looking back I see where I went wrong
So now the cycle I must break
I need to right the wrongs of my past
So the initiative I now take

I will be a positive role model
And good advice I will exchange
To the youth who feel they have no hope
And to those who think they cannot change

Don't see yourselves as victims of society
Drs, Artists and Scientists you can be
You need to know you're worth so much more
How others have made it, take a look and see

I spent less and less time around gang members
And avoided places they would be
I didn't answer their calls or text messages
But looked out for my family

Of course I was threatened and bullied
But still I stood my ground
They made it hard for me to leave
But to them I was not bound

I came to the realisation
That this was not the life for me
Shootings, stabbings and a life of crime
From all this I wanted to be free

They told me I'd have no protection
They threatened my friends and family too
They tried everything to make me stay
But building up the courage to leave was my biggest breakthrough

So I made it out
And you can too
It may not be that easy
But it's not impossible to do

© 2016

I MADE THE RIGHT CHOICE

Nuff of my friends
Aren't around anymore
They listened to others
And then opened the wrong door

I was under a lot of pressure
And I didn't know what to do
I had no education, money or a job
I really didn't have a clue

I couldn't go clubbing
And I couldn't go out for a meal
I couldn't buy myself new clothes
And it became a big deal

Sometimes I didn't even have bus fare
Many times I felt so low
I often thought about making easy money
But through that door I couldn't go.

Nuff of my friends
Aren't around anymore
There dead or in prison
Because they wanted to live rich, not poor

The temptations all around me
No education, no job, no home
Just drugs, drink and criminals
I felt so all alone

I didn't give up though
I had to stand my ground
I had to fight through the pressure
And now a good job I've found

It's tough out there on the streets
And only the fittest will survive
And not by any means necessary
I had to make the right choice to stay alive

So how did I do It, I hear you ask
With nuff determination and strong will
I had to separate myself from certain people
And the negative thoughts I had to kill

I had to believe that I was better than that
And so I wasn't about to go break the law
I had to make some positive choices
Because nuff of my friends aren't around anymore.

© 2015

BE THANKFUL

Be thankful for life
Even though at times it may be hard
Make the changes you want to see
It normally begins in your own backyard.

What do I mean by that?
Well it normally starts with you
Don't worry about Joe Bloggs down the road
Be accountable for what you do.

Be thankful for others
For love and support you receive
Be thankful for your blessings
In luck I just don't believe.

Be thankful for peace
And when in those moments you can reflect
Because life is what you make it
So negative thoughts you need to reject.

Be thankful for joy and happiness
And all the things that make you smile
Try and think positive thoughts
Even if, it only lasts for a while.

Be thankful for all you have
You have more than you know
Be thankful for today
You can only reap the seeds you sow.

Thank you.
March 2022

HOPE FOR 2022

A new year begins
I look forward to it with hope
So many things and lives have changed
But we're strong, so that's how we'll cope.
I hope for shorter NHS waiting lists

And that hospital visits will be reinstated
For no more talk of the dreaded virus
Or, for the whole world to be vaccinated.

I hope for peace and normality
I want to live not merely survive
It's about love, joy and happiness
And for that we all must strive.

I just want to see people smiling
And to say hello as we pass each other by
I want to see children playing happily
I want to see rainbows in the sky.

I hope that people will get the help they need
In sickness and in health
Communities need to come together
No matter the power or the wealth.

My hope is to be reunited
With all my friends and family
I want to hug and not just shake hands
I'm sure most of you will all agree.

Agree that there needs to be a change
We need to be positive and mindful of each other
We need to show love and care
And not just shrug our shoulders and say we can't bother.

So be confident in all you do
Challenge and commit yourselves to be great
And make your dreams come true
Because, that's my Hope, for 2022.

FEB 2022

HOW TO BE CONFIDENT

Tell yourself that you're beautiful/handsome and strong
And always act in a positive way
Let go of negative thoughts
And get to know yourself today.

Action breeds confidence and courage
Life's not about pleasing others all the time
It's about being true to you
Even if the corporate ladder you want to climb.

Believe in yourself, you're in control
Hold your head up high and smile
Even when others around you are losing theirs
Stay calm; this will raise your profile.

Think positive, think positive
Because it's all in your mind
Believe you are capable at all times
And your confidence you will find.

You are confident.

Nov 2016

HOW TO BE HAPPY

Occupy your mind with positive thoughts
Be satisfied and content
Surround yourself with friends and loved ones
As this is often time well spent

Take care of yourself
Be a little more active each day
They'll be setbacks, challenges and roadblocks
But don't let these get in your way.

Do your best to make yourself happy
By doing what you love the most
Whether it's cooking, writing or dancing
Or travelling from coast to coast.

Look for positives in every experience
Control your thoughts and feelings too
Meditate, pray or spiritually reflect
But never give up on you.

Happiness is that feeling when you know life is good
And that's what makes you smile
It's time to enjoy your life
Even if but for a while.

Don't worry, Be Happy.

Nov 2016

I HOPE

What am I hoping for?
That the sun will shine on you
That you'll celebrate your life
And give thanks in all you do.

What am I hoping for?
That you'll smile as you continue to read
That you'll realise your life is precious
And that you have much more than you need.

What am I hoping for?
That you know how strong you are
That you're blessed and loved by God
And that's the greatest gift by far.

Hope It's your guide and path to happiness
It allows you to see what can be
It's expecting something to happen
And without it, we would not be.

Hope, It's having a desire, a wish and a dream
It's being optimist in your mind
It's about never giving up
Otherwise you will be left behind.

It allows you to approach problems
With a mind-set suitable to success
It opens doors to find a way out of a problem
At a time when you're feeling distress.

Hope It's all you need to keep on living
It's a single candle burning in the night
It creates endurance and strength
It brings you out of darkness and into light.

And that's my Hope for you.

Nov 2nd

WHAT IS HOPE?

It's your guide and path to happiness
It allows you to see what could be
It's expecting something to happen
And without it, I wouldn't be me.

It's having a desire, a wish and a dream
It's being optimistic in your mind
It's about never giving up
Because if you do, you'll be left behind.

It allows you to approach problems
With a mindset suitable for success
It opens doors to find a way out of a problem
At a time when you're feeling distress.

It's all you need to keep on living
It's a single candle burning in the night
It creates endurance and strength
It brings you out of darkness and into light.

That's my hope for you.

Nov 2020

YOU INSPIRE ME

Today you should make life count
Because yesterday matters no more
Tomorrow is not promised
So this moment is the only moment in life that's sure.

Today you should make life count
So smile whenever you can
Spread love and be kind to others
Whether you are a child, woman or man.

You inspire me to make life count
I only have this life to live
So I'll be content with all I have for now
And my love to others I'll give.

Inspired by Clinton. 2017

YES YOU CAN

What's on your mind?
Have you expressed that idea?
Do you know what to do?
Or are you thoughts still unclear?

You can do it
You have the potential
Find the people who are positive
And not the ones that are judgmental.

You can do it
You just need to persevere
You need to believe in yourself
To make that dream of yours appear.

You can do it, yes you can
But Rome was not built in a day
You need to have endurance
When it does not happen straight away.

Only you can make it happen
Others can only help you so far
Believing is the key to achieving
To you becoming that superstar.

You can do it.

June 2016

CHAPTER TWO

LIFE

"You will face many defeats in your life but never let yourself be defeated"

"When someone shows you who they are, believe them the first time"

By Mayo Angelou

ELAINE GIBBONS

THE WAITING ROOM

Here I sit
Just waiting to hear
The anticipation is too much
It's really more than I can bare
I'm hoping it's going to be good news
Not sure what I'll do if it's bad
Not sure if I should feel indifferent
Or whatever the news, be glad
Different conversations around me
As the people come and go
We're all waiting for an answer
But each other we don't know
Emotions and thoughts
And hearts beating fast
Imaginations running wild
How long will these last?
I got here early
But don't know when I'll leave
Not sure who is in front of me
But I'm up next I do believe
Others were not so lucky
As they left the waiting room
Stifled cries and half dried tears
And expressions of doom and gloom

The waiting room can be a dreadful place
For any age, sex, colour, creed or race

It has no respect
But a little patient care
I know most of the people
Would rather not be there

Doctors, dentists, consultants or nurse
They can be a blessing, but also a curse

I'm really sick of waiting in this waiting room.

© 2014

WHAT A SHAME

I see nothings changed
In fact it's a whole lot worse
More homeless people on the street
Is the shortage of housing their only curse?
According to statistics
There's 100 evictions everyday
The bailiffs arrive with warrants
To take their homes or possessions away.
Food bank vouchers
For those on the poverty line
Great Britain was once thriving
But it's now gone way back in time.
Poverty stricken cities
You could face famine or a flood
Wars and terrorism
And people killing in cold blood.
Are the rich getting richer?
As the poor live in disbelief
Politicians say no more recession
But I see no progress or relief.
In this modern day society
The cost of living's above the average wage
Many live without gas and electricity
How can that be in this day and age?
How can we solve these problems?
Where do the answers lie?
Do we continue to blame the government?
While many sit back and sigh?

The majority have spoken
Surely not, I hear them say
We all have to be responsible
Because no one wants to live this way.

© 2016

CHILDREN

Some say they're a blessing
But some are labelled as a curse
Many grow up level headed
But some become so much worse.
Our children are killing children
Some have no respect at all
Their parents can't control them
So by the wayside many fall.
But you can't be your child's friend
You have to teach discipline, boundaries and respect
You shouldn't spoil them rotten
Otherwise your responsibilities you'll neglect.
You have to learn to say no
And mean what you say
There's no time for double standards
Or you'll be sorry someday.
They'll scream and shout
Some will say they hate you
They'll threaten to go live with grandma
Or friends and other relatives too.
But never give them the upper hand
Because they are only children
As parents you must have the last word
Whilst doing your best for them
These children are our future
So we need to grow them right
There's never been a manual
So try with all your might.

To do the very best you can
They'll be ups and downs along the way
But persevere with love and care
But to never give up, I hope you'll swear.

© 2016

UNEXPLAINED FEELINGS

Sometimes I just don't know
I really don't know how I feel
Am I confused, depressed or afraid?
Am I going thru this for real?
I've got a good job
A house that's all mine
Friends and family that love me
And so I really haven't got time
To think too deep upon these feelings
Or let the haters get in my way
Because I know there trying to weigh me down
But I won't let them lead me astray
They can take you to a place
Where you really don't want to be
Things will appear before you
That you really don't want to see.
Those thoughts are dark
And full of despair
They'll tell you no-one loves you
And for others you don't care
They'll make you angry
By telling you lies
Over and over again
Those negative thoughts rise
They can take over your mind
But you can't let them win
You must stay positive

And find the strength within
The strength to rise above those feelings
Because giving in would be just wrong
There's light at the end of the tunnel
So stay positive and strong

©2014

TRAFFIC

I just want to get home
But there's traffic ahead
Drivers beeping their horns
I wish they'd be patient instead.
The old lady crossing the road
5 yards from the zebra crossing
Why do they always do that?
As I shake my head laughing.
Drivers on their mobile phones
Didn't notice the lights turned green
Angry drivers pointing at them
That's against the law… I hear them scream.
Three buses in a row
So I try and come out of that queue
But no-one will give me way
So I just sit there and screw.
I give other drivers way
And always let them pass
Without not even a thank you
I promise that will be the last.
Common courtesy don't cost
As we all go about our day
They can't get much further up the road
Even if they speed away.
I'm stuck in traffic
Because someone's broken down
There's been an accident, I'm diverted

That's why I wear this frown
I just want to get home
I wish I could fly
I'll just have to ride it out
I'm stuck in traffic… that's why.

Inspired by Bentley Noble
© 2016

HE GOT IT WRONG

We made no plans
So I went out with a mate
It was a night to remember
But certainly not a date.
I loved you like a brother
You were my best friend
You said I hurt your feelings
And so it all came to an end
I couldn't have known how you felt
I could not have read your mind
I could not predict your deepest thoughts
But now know love is truly blind
I was blind to how you truly felt
Your feelings ran real deep
You've thrown our friendship away
Even though you had my heart to keep
I loved you, but lost you
A better friend I'll never find
I'll never forget you
You were always loving and so kind
You really got it so wrong
But never let me explain
Two hearts have now been broken
And two of us are now in pain
I still can't believe it
As I sit here and cry
You said I did nothing wrong

So I'm still wondering why
Why you would leave me
And throw our friendship away
I have nothing more to give
And I have nothing more to say.

© 2014

LONELINESS

It ain't a joke
You have to feel it to know
Isolated, abandoned or rejected
You just feel so low.
Day in, day out and it's just you
And you feel so all alone
You've got kids, you got family
But they're living their lives now that they're grown.
Some say get a pet or hobby
But find something to do
That's easier said than done
You're not the one walking in my shoe.
It ain't a joke
Eating, sleeping and waking alone
With just the T.V for company
Or a conversation on the phone.
It makes you question yourself
And it's bound to make you cry
You know you've done nothing wrong
But still you wonder why.
You try and work through it
By keeping as busy as you can
We all go through it at some stage
Whether you're a woman or a man.
It ain't a joke
You can feel lonely in a crowd
It can be hard to admit
Especially when you say it out loud.

It's a painful awareness
Not to feel connected to another
It's not about having lots of friends
Because to some that just don't matter.
It's about feeling that no-one cares for you
It's about feeling you don't belong
It's about feeling sad
When you here that certain song.
But don't be downhearted
It won't always be like this
You will find that special person
And will live a life of bliss.

Inspired by David Skins

© 2016

WHAT MAKES ME HAPPY

Seeing a brand new day
Because it's a blessing from God
Having health and strength
As onward I plod.
Seeing the beauty of God's creation
Feeling the sun on my black skin
I may have trials and tribulations
But have peace and love within.
Knowing that I am strong and independent
Giving thanks for the foundation laid
Thank you God for mom and dad
And the sacrifices they made.
My children, brothers and sisters
And the love and support we share
My grandson, nephew and nieces too
And knowing they'll always be there.
Giving thanks and praise to the almighty
The keeper of my soul
Who's given me hope in heaven
So to reach there is my goal.

What makes me Truly Happy?
Is the fact that I am blessed
I have nothing to worry about
In a world that's just so stressed.

© 2016

WHERE'S MY BOYFRIEND?

I woke up this morning alone
No tea and toast by my bed
I couldn't get him on the phone
Where's my boyfriend?

I go to work and what a day
I come home to dirty dishes
So once again you'll hear me say
Where's my boyfriend?

Tidy up and cook our dinner
Begin to chill
I think I'm on to a winner
But where's my boyfriend?

I light the candles and patiently wait
No text or call to say he's running late
Where's my boyfriend?

He told me he was working today
And was much too busy to stop
But as I was driving down the road
I saw him going into the betting shop
Oh there's my boyfriend
There's my boyfriend

Inspired by David Skins

© 2016

OUR COMMUNITY

We are to love our community
And respect where we live
We are to come together
And be more proactive
We are a community
There should be none greater than we
In numbers we are powerful
And that's the way it ought to be
We need to improve our schools
Our businesses and homes
Without getting into debt
Or relying on payday loans
We need to grow up our children
In a loving community
We need to teach them how to live
In peace and harmony
Encouragement sweetens labour
Our community needs to stand strong
We can't give up on each other
We have to prove our oppressors wrong
If we all look around
Tell me what it is you see?
Everyone else is progressing
Except our community
We don't all have to struggle
Our forefathers set us free
We need to see Martin Luther's dream

But it's not apparent in this country
We need to change those mindsets
Who don't believe we can live in peace
We need to be united
So all community wars can one day cease.

© 2014

LORD I'M TIRED

Thank God it's Friday
And the weekend is here
I don't work on Saturday
But my work don't stop there

Lord I'm tired
But I have housework to do
I've got children to take care of
And my man's food to cook too

Lord I'm tired
I've food to go and buy
Clothes to go and wash
Oh Lord tell me why

Why we women
Need to be so strong
Keep the house, and the children
And still take care of a man

Go to work
To keep ourselves fed
Come home to more work
And still be wicked in bed

We try keep in shape
And look after our hair
We wear nice clothes
Men… try disagreeing if you dare

We look after our parents
And not just our own
We look after the grandchildren
Even when their parents still live at home

We look after
Our brothers and sisters too
The dog, the cat
All without, a thank you

We smile, we nod
Say yes when we should say no
And even when we're tired and weary
We still find time though

To multi-task and juggle
And just to keep the peace
Lord knows that we're tired
So men applaud your women, please

We do all this
Because we love and care
Lord knows that we're tired
And we know life isn't fair

Men show a little love
And a lot of attention
You will reap the rewards
In which department I won't mention

But if we're happy
Men you know you will be too
You will get the best of us
But how much is up to you

Lord knows that I'm tired
But I love my little life
Being an independent women
Mother, partner, friend and wife

I'm counting my blessings
Because I'm here to tell the tale
That when we run and become weary
We may stumble but never fail

Because in the eyes of God we're strong
But in the heart of man, we're weak
Our strength comes from above
So God's face I'll always seek

So ladies do what you love
And love what you do
Because even when your tired
The good Lord will always bless you.

© 2014

NATURE

If it doesn't rain, it pours
That's just one of nature's laws
The sun will shine but it's still cold
Some of us will feel it more, especially if we're old.
Hail and thunder
Even lighting may strike
We'll all run for cover
Because that weather we dislike.
The clouds will cover over
The blueness of the sky
The moon will light the darkness
And the sun will set on high.
These are the makings of God
The one and only creator
If we put our trust in him
He will bless us and show his favour.

© 2016

HATERS

They're mean and ugly
and their blood runs cold
they're jealous of everyone
whether you're young or you're old.
They will have a smile on their face
as they stab you in the back
they could be Asian, White or Black.
Misery loves company
so they won't want you to succeed
they will try and hold you back
but stand up and take the lead.
They'll dislike you for no reason
but just because you're you
and the fact that you get on with life
while they have nothing better to do.
They'll be hostile, repelled and revolted
at the thought of your success
they'll be nothing you can do about it
because about themselves they feel much less.
they'll be resentful, jealous and envious
of your achievements, possessions and looks
they'll emulate your every move
and try and stay in your good books.
if you recognise them, run them
get rid of and dismiss
these people mean you no good at all
especially if you live a life of bliss.

(c)2016

FORGIVE THEM

I'm not asking you to forget what happened
It's not a pardon or excuse for what they've done
You don't have to include them in your life
But if you don't forgive them, they'll have won.

Forgiveness is about YOU, not them
Because it will allow YOU to heal
It will give YOU a peace of mind
And that's exactly what YOU need to feel.

Try to Forgive even if you can't forget.

Written by Elaine Gibbons

2016

HE WAS DEPRESSED

Hell on earth
Is how he described his life
he said he had no hope
Because he'd just separated from his children and wife.

He was no longer the breadwinner
And felt he could no longer provide
Security for his family
All he was left with was his pride.

In his flat he'd cook a meal for one
In front of the TV he'd sit alone
He felt family and friends had abandoned him
Because no one would call his phone.

He spent a lot of time thinking
Because it began to get real deep
Thoughts of the mistakes he'd made
And the promises he did not keep.

For weeks he would not venture out
He said he had nowhere to go
The shame of having nothing
Left him feeling very low.

Anxiety and Depression
Is what the Dr had said
The neighbours all agreed
They were the ones that found him dead.

He'd taken an overdose of pills
And left a departing letter
It said "I'm sorry for all the pain I've caused
But this way I feel, is better".

My message is do not suffer in silence.

ELAINE GIBBONS

WATCH YOUR MOUTH

The words we speak are powerful
They can hurt or raise a smile
They can damage or encourage
Or make you stop and think a while.

The words we speak are powerful
So be careful what you say
You can't take it back once spoken
Especially if it's taken in the wrong way.

The words we speak are powerful
Here is an example to name a few
Mohammed Ali and Nelson Mandela
Martin Luther King and Desmond Tutu.

The words they spoke were powerful
And they stood for what they believed
They left a legacy behind
The world can see what they've achieved.

The words we speak are so powerful
So need to be used in the right way
Do your words help or hinder?
Will mine make you stop and think today?

Inspired by David Skins

June 2016

WHO AM I?

Who am i?

I am a child of God, trying to live the best that I can,

According to his word.

Who am I?

I am an independent woman and mother of two adult children.

I am a very proud grandmother.

Who am I?

I am a daughter, sister and friend

I try to be supportive, trustworthy, respectful and loyal.

Who am I?

I am my reflection in the mirror and I am the truth in my heart.

Inspired by Clinton. 2017

CHAPTER THREE

LOVE

"Love recognizes no barriers. It jumps hurdles, leaps fences, penetrates walls to arrive at its destination full of hope"

By Mayo Angelou

WHAT IS IT?

Everyone wants it
Sometimes it's hard to find
But it's such a beautiful thing
That God gave to mankind.
It keeps us alive
It can make us strong
Some say it's blind
But how can it be wrong?
It's a variety of feelings
An emotion of strong attraction
Some say it's unconditional
But also leaves many heartbroken.
It warms the heart
When it feels a connection
But can be cold and lonely
When faced with rejection.
It goes along way
And is said to conquer all
It has no boundaries
So how deep can we fall?
Some say it makes the world go round
And its not suppose to hurt
But when my heart aches
The pain I can't divert.
But for whatever reason
It's a feeling we all enjoy
And that's why each others heart
We should aim never to destroy.

IT'S LOVE

© 2016

My Mom

You're like a ray of sunshine
And a light of hope
Without your love and support
I don't know how I'd ever cope
You're never too busy
And nothing's ever too much
You're always there when I need you
With your tender loving touch
You've been a wonderful example
Of how a Mother should be
I want to tell you that I love you
For everything you've done for me
We've shared many happy moments
We've laughed, we've smiled, we've cried
I promise to show appreciation
As long as I have you by my side
Mother dear Mother
What more can I say,
I hope you have a wonderful
And Happy Mothers Day.

Everyday is Mothers Day
Written with my mom in mind

© 2015

I LOVE HER

You care for me when I'm weak
And build me up to make me strong
You dry my tears and make me smile
You've always taught me right from wrong
You've always set a good example
And always told the truth to me
Without your love, advice and guidance
I really don't know were I'd be.
Love is what you've given me
Because love is all you know
You've been a wonderful Mother
And I really love you so.
You've been a tower of strength
You're always here for me
Your love is unconditional
For everyone to see
Your kind and thoughtful
With a heart made of gold
I hope to be like you some day
If the truth is to be told
You're gracious and humble
I just want to say I love you too
I wish you all the very best for today
And joy and happiness in all you do.

© 2015

WHEN YOU LOVE SOMEONE

When she's in love
She gives her whole heart
When she knows she's loved
You'll find it hard to be apart.
She makes you feel wanted
And will do the best she can
To make you feel needed
It won't be a part of any plan.
She's just naturally loving
And knows just how to please
In the kitchen and the bedroom
She'll add some spice and a little tease.
With good principles and values
She'll help to raise the children right
Her family will always come first
And she'll always have her man in sight.
To love and protect
And to defend whenever she can
Some women would say, why do that
And she'll say, cos he's my man.
He gives her what she needs
He supports and respects her too
He's caring, loving and loyal
And never tells her what to do.
When you love someone don't try change them
Just love them and let them grow
Just remember why you fell in love
And the rest in time will show.

Men are from Mars and women are from Venus
We two can never be the same
It takes patience and understanding
To play the relationship game.
So take time to compromise
And listen to each other
Take each others feelings into consideration
And your love might last forever.

© 2015

MY VALENTINE

I love you with all that I am
My mind, my body and soul
I knew no love before you
So now you've made me whole.
I love you for your tenderness
Your thoughtfulness and care
I knew long ago you where the one for me
So with you my heart I'll share.
No matter what we go through
You're always there for me
You're never judgemental or ready to blame
It's just my goodness that you see.
I owe you so much
For coming into my life
You always make me happy
And you've been a wonderful wife.

Happy Valentines Day

©2016

MY FATHER

My Father is
A good man, a teacher and friend
You are always there for me
And on you I can depend
You taught me to have manners and respect
You taught me to work hard and be strong
You taught me to lead and not follow
Even when things go wrong
You always said to have ambition
And to be positive in life
You always told me that a bigger man will know
Just when to walk away from strife
You always tell me to do the best I can
And try to help others along the way
I just hope that you are proud of me
As I hope the best for you today.

© 2016

My Love and I

You are my soul mate
You're more than a friend to me
From the first time we met
My I, became we
We two became one
As we fell in love
I hope we have many years together
We've been blessed by God above
You make me happy
And you make me smile
You help me forget about my worries
Even if but for a while
I feel safe in your arms
As I dare to dream
That our love will last forever
I am the cat that got the cream
I feel so blessed
To be loved by you
You give me all that I need
And I really love you too
I thank the Dear Lord
For bringing us together
I pray you'll be my Valentine
For now and forever.

© 2016

ELAINE GIBBONS

SHE'S BLESSED

I just want to say I love you
And thanks for being my mom
There's so much more I want to say
But I'm not sure where to start from
You've been there since my beginning
And say you'll be there to the end
No matter what we go through
You'll be my Mother and my friend
We spend many days together
And talk for hours on the phone
We keep each other company
So we don't have to be alone
These words are just for you
There's so much more that I can say
But I just want to wish you
A very happy Mothers Day.

Everyday is Mothers Day

© 2015

A FATHER AND SON

A father is to be there for his baby
A father is to be there for his child
A father is to be there when he's grown
Even if he's not meek or mild
A father is to be a good example
A father is to show him love and care
A father is to know how to communicate with his son
And let him know he'll always be there
A father is to teach him how to be a good man
A father is to teach him manners and respect
A father is to teach him how to love women
And how his family he must always protect
A father doesn't have to related by blood
A father just needs to be strong
A father needs to be able to come correct
And admit at times when he's wrong
A son needs his father
So father thank you for doing the best you can
Thank you for good principles and good values
Thank you for teaching me how to be a good man.

© 2016

ELAINE GIBBONS

My One and Only

We've shared so much together
And you are my better half
At times when I've felt oh so low
You knew how to make me laugh
You've always stood by my side
And said you'd never give up on me
Our love has stood the test of time
Without you, where would I be?
Your patience is overwhelming
You're caring and so kind
You're always thinking of others
A better wife I could not find
I may not tell you often
But I appreciate all you do
I'll do anything to make you happy
Because I have always loved you too
So be my Valentine today
And my Valentine tomorrow
I hope you liked the Red Rose
That I left this morning on your pillow.

© 2016

JUST LET ME

I just want to love you
And not take anything from you
I just want to care for you
I don't want to change you
I just want to be the one you want
I don't want to stress you
I just want your company
I don't want to stop you
I just want to hear from you
I don't want you to stop talking
I just want to share my life with you
I don't want to hold you down
I just want to build you up
I just want you to show that you care
I want all that you said you wanted
I don't want you to misunderstand me
I want you to hear me loud and clear
I don't want you to be under no illusion
I want you to know that I mean what I say
I don't want your words without actions
I want you to know that I'm real
I don't want to force you into something new
I just want you to know how much
I love you, just let me

Inspired by "the story of his life"

© 2016

WHAT YOU MEAN TO ME

F.   Friendly, firm but funny

A.   Approachable, adorable and awesome

T.   Talented, thoughtful and treasured

H.   Handsome, helpful and honest

E.   Educated, excellent and encouraging

R.   Reliable, reasonable and real

Everyday is Fathers Day, I love you

© 2016

WHAT I REALLY THINK

You are a charmer with a ring of truth
You have more life experience, but I have my youth
I have more energy and more time
You have your thoughts, but check out my rhyme
We had an instant attraction
That quickly blew my mind
You were a few steps ahead
As I was slow to unwind
We shared something's in common
But still we did not fit
As I tried to express my feelings
You'd only listen for a bit
We eventually came together
We found some common ground
We decided to give us a chance
Now love between us can be found.

© 2016

ELAINE GIBBONS

TO LOVE, YOU AND ME

It's when you come into a room
It's when I smell your sweet perfume
It makes my heart smile
And not just now, but all the while.
I think of you and I go crazy
The things you do always seem to amaze me
Your hearts so big and always giving
You're a part of me, for you I'm living.
Your love is like no other I've known
It's always been there, but I can see that it's grown.
I love your smile and eyes as well
I look into your soul and I can tell
That you're a genuine man with no hidden agenda
So I love you now, and will forever
I'll be all that you need me to be
You won't have to wonder, cos I'll make you see
That I am the one, your one and only
It will be us two so you'll never be lonely.

Love, its kind, that's you
Love is always compassionate too
Love, it's what we all need
Love…. I hope I've planted that seed.

© 2016

SHE LOVES HIM

She wants a man
But not if him a go mean
Cos she will wash an cook fe him
Jus fe keep him keen.

She just want somebody fe love har
Cos she kno she have a good heart
She want a fardda fe har pickney dem
Right from de very start.

So, she meet dis man tree weeks ago
And him tek har pon jus one date
No him a tark bout him wha move in
Me tell har she fe mek him wait.

Wait til him mek a commitment
Wait til she get de ring
She fe wait til she meet him family dem
And den she cyan claim har king.

No she seh she love him
So stop watch arl de tv soap dem
Instead she watch documentary and Texas Ranger
And stop hang wid har girlfren dem.

She tell me seh she cut him toe nail dem
And squeeze di bump pon him head
And even tho him nah work at all
Every marning him get breakfast in bed.

She love him

She seh him good wid de pickney dem
Cos him tek dem go a park
But dem seh a dem push him pon de swing
Me tell har she a skylark

Cos how you fe have a man weh jus a tek tek
An nah give you nuttin at all
But when Valentines Day cum an you no get nuttin
You deh pon de phone a barl.

Me arsk har what present she buy him
She seh 2 pants, 2 shirt and 2 shoes
Me arsk har if she no mad
She seh no, dats jus what him choose.

She love him

Me arsk har if him help roun de house
She seh no, him seh him have a bad back
Me arsk har if him a look fe any work
She seh no, not since him get de sack.

Me arsk is what she get outta de relationship
She seh him love har in him own way
She seh him jus misundastood
And she hoping to become him wife one day.

Hush, she love him.

Well, as much as me no agree wid some a dem ting deh
Is me girlfren so me affe put har right
But me nah get between no man an him woman
Cos me no wha dem fe seh me cause dem fe fight.

So love who unnu wha fe love
But no mek nobody tek unnu fe fool
Cos you firs affe love youself
And dats de golden rule.

CHAPTER FOUR
MY GOD

"While I know myself as a creation of God, I am also obligated to realize and remember that everyone else and everything else are also Gods creation"

By Mayo Angelou

ELAINE GIBBONS

THERE'S NO ONE LIKE HIM

I love you because you love me
You've promised to never leave
I love you because you first loved me
And that I truly believe
I love you because you give me strength
When I've had none of my own
I love you because you've never failed me yet
Even at times when I've felt alone
I love you because you keep your promises
And your word is always true
I love you because you're forgiving
And I can always count on you
I love you because you protect me
And turn things around for my good
I love you because you guide me
And help me to live the way I should
Your love is overwhelming
And you're always here to comfort me
You answer when I call
Even though your face I cannot see
So I promise to stay connected
And I promise to stay true
I promise to persevere
In all that I go through
You bring the right people in my life
And open doors no man can close
You are the source of my survival
And out of many it's me you chose.

All you ask is for me to be faithful
And to serve you to the end
To keep all your commandments
Thank you Lord for being my friend

©2015

THE ONE

My God is faithful
He is my best friend
He will never leave me comfortless
But will guide me to the end.
My God is faithful
He say's he'll never leave me alone
He is so faithful
Out of many I am his own
He is so faithful
He say's he'll catch me if I fall.
My God is faithful
So in him I put my trust
He's never failed me yet
So to love him is a must.
He is the joy of my salvation
And the peace within my soul
He is the one I can depend on
And the one who makes me whole.
He is the source of my survival
And the only one I need
He's the way, the truth and life
And through him I will succeed.
My God is truly faithful
And as his servant I will be too
My God is truly awesome
Without him what would I do?

© 2015

WHY I PRAY

I pray because I have faith
I pray because I believe
I pray because my God says,
If I ask I will receive.
I pray because it comforts me
To know I have a friend
Who lives within my heart
And whose love will never end.
I pray because it works for me
I know it carries power
I've proved it time and time again
And not just in my darkest hour.
I pray every morning and at night
And talk to God in between
He's promised never to leave me
So he's a part of my daily routine.
I pray Dear Lord
To live according to your word
And will continue to pray
Because I know I'll always be heard.

© 2016

DEAR LORD

Thank you for waking me up this morning
And for seeing me on my way
I hope you'll go before me
As I go through the rest of this day.
I hope to be loving, kind and patient
And keep a smile upon my face
I want to do good onto others
No matter what creed, colour or race.
Please use me to be a blessing
To someone who has a need
In a world that lacks peace and love
I pray I will succeed.
Thank you in advance Lord
For blessings great and small
Because no matter what I go through
You promise to see me though it all.

© April 2016

HOW GOOD IS GOD?

Well, he woke me up this morning
And put a smile back on my face
He has never left me comfortless
So in my heart he has a place.
I can feel his love within me
It's just like a peaceful glow
In wish all mankind could feel it
I wish I could let the whole world know.
What it is to have him as my friend
He takes me as I am
I try and put him before all things
He's a part of my daily plan.
So put your trust in Jesus
When you kneel down to pray
Ask all things in his name
And then let him lead the way.
He will love you like no other
He wants to give you nothing but the best
All he asks is that you follow him
Have faith and he'll do the rest.
So Thank You God for Jesus
And for all you've done for me
If I didn't have you in my life
I really don't know where I'd be.

© 2009

PLEASE GOD

Please God guide me
And teach me your way
Help me to be obedient
So I don't have to go astray.
Please God give me courage
So I can do your will
And give me daily strength
At times when I need to be still.
Please God help me to do what's right
So that I can be a blessing too
So that I can love and encourage others
To stand up and follow you.

© 2009

CHAPTER FIVE
REALITY

"History despite its wrenching pain, cannot be unlived, but if faced with courage, need not be lived again"

"You may not control all the events that happen to you, but you can decide not to be reduced by them"

"The best part of life is not just surviving, but thriving with passion and compassion and humour and style and generosity and kindness"

By Mayo Angelou

CRIMES AGAINST HUMANITY

I can feel the energy
The love and support as I breathe
I'm not about to do the track and trace
There's that look again upon your face.

Who are you trying to find?
Who are you trying to control?
As if I don't know it's all about your end goal
To vaccinate and depopulate
And even when you make it mandatory, I won't be taking it, mate.

I've got rights, I'm a human being
So step off my neck
You're being watched, you're being see
As thousands of us die, of Covid19.

Society's elite and the Government
Are the powers that shouldn't be
They want a New World Order
But nobody asked me.

You can't control,
Dictate or oppress me
I can see it in your eyes
The lies and the misery
The way you stammer, back track and lay blame
Onto the innocent communities
I think it's a bloody shame.

Them and their two metre distance
Masks and curfews
They're trying to separate humanity
But we will protest, and they will lose.

Misinformation in the mainstream media
As they drive home constant fear
As if Covid19 is the only news
Negativity has been notched up a gear.

The worlds at a standstill
But Covid19s on the rise
Or so they'd like the world to believe
With their bullshit stories, and their blatant lies.

They're trying to control the way we work
The economy and health system
Our education and our social interaction
If I had a gun, I would pistol whip them.

Yes, I do believe they've engineered this virus
It's a plandemic created for their purpose
It's a global crime against humanity
These people are wicked and very ruthless.

It makes sense to me
But may not to you
But I'm hoping my rhymes will open some eyes
So all of the people don't have to be hypnotised.

ELAINE GIBBONS

They made movies predicting Covid19 would happen
Called Dead Plague and Contagion in 2011
None of this was a coincidence
They were preparing us for what was to happen.

Don't get it twisted, it's true
It was a rehearsal for the future
The authorities want to take control
As they prepare for the New World Order.

The virus may have originated in China
But the process began many years before
With Bill Gates investing Millions in vaccines
He wants to depopulate the world for sure

They've committed crimes against humanity
But I will continue to pray
That the truth will be revealed
For all to see someday.

Too many lives ruined
And so many lives lost
We can't let them get away with it
What other freedoms will it cost?

Oct 2020

LIFE ON LOCKDOWN

The Government said I couldn't spend time with my mother
My brothers, sisters or kids
They say I can only go out for food
They're trying to tell me how to exit.

They didn't give me life
And they can't control me
With Covid 19 and lockdowns
Or with their lies and exaggerated story.

We had to queue outside shops
Social distance is the new word
Washing hands is the second
And wearing masks is the third.

Let's not forget about PPE
Test and trace and the vaccine
The good old NHS
And the ventilation machine.

But worst of all, so many lives lost
And others who died alone
With loved ones not able to say goodbye
And with last requests unknown.

Black people can't have a nine night
And we can't attend a funeral
They've locked down our church
Because they know that we're spiritual.

They're spreading fear amongst the people
With bad vibes, fake news and no hope
Spreading lies, lies, and more lies
Making you wonder how you going to cope.

If you don't social distance
And refuse the vaccine
They will make it mandatory
Or you'll be forced to live in quarantine.

On lockdown you didn't need to get dressed
Because for days you had nowhere to go
I had no need to fill up on petrol
I worked from home, many was on furlough.

In the shops there was no toilet roll
Hand sanitizers, eggs or flour
Most shelves were nearly empty
Anyone would think they were all on offer.

People were just going crazy
It was about panic buying
A nurse couldn't get any fruit after a long shift
She was on the TV the next day crying.

So many thousands lost their jobs
Many businesses forced to close
So many people still suffering
When will this end……only God knows.

May 2020

LIFE

Life is precious
Life is a blessing
Life is a gift from God
So please stop stressing.

Please try not to complain
Mumble or groan
In life you get what you give
And reap the seeds that you have sown.

Be thankful and content
Try and change the things you can
But what you can't change leave it to God
Because he is the creator of all man.

Love yourself
And love others too
Live for today
Because tomorrow's, not promised to you.

Nov 2016

ELAINE GIBBONS

My View On Lockdown

I saw things that were always there
But that I'd never seen before
It's been my garden for 14 years
But this is the time to explore.

The squirrels, the birds
The ants and the flies
The white and grey clouds
And the beautiful clear skies.

Flowers blossomed in the grass
Everything grew and became
I was looking out of my window
Straight into a picture frame.

I watched as the nightime developed
With nothing to obstruct my view
I was blessed to see the morning unfolding
As the light from the sun made it through.

Autumn ended and spring began
I'm finally taking time to see
The sheer beauty of God's creation
I'm right where I want to be.

I have a room with a view
Time to reflect and think
The lockdown had done me a favour
As the days seem to interlink.

I have a room with a view
I do count myself as blessed
The foxes, the cats, the dog barking next door
The children playing in the garden
I didn't really hear all that before.

I'd count the Magpies landing
First one, two then three
I saw the little Robin on my fence
Whilst the wind blows through the tree.

I saw things that were always there
But that I'd never seen before
Life is truly beautiful
Even if at times a little unsure.

With so many lives lost
And so much heartache and pain
Will things ever go back?
To being normal again?

May 2020

MEN

Men …..So let me tell you what I know about you
I don't' know that much… ok maybe a thing or two
You big, strong, confident and bold
You like to take charge and share stories untold.
You like your gadgets and fancy cars
You like going to parties and cocktail bars.
You open doors and let us ladies in first
But if your fade don't set right, you're ready to curse.

But some of unnu….. Lard unnu wicked is a shame
Unnu treat unnu women bad, and refuse to tek de blame
And at home, nuff of unnu different you see, no air and graces anymore
Unnu don't even put down de toilet seat
And leave unnu dirty towel on de bathroom floor.
Unnu won't even help unnu partner wash up de two plate
Or even put out de rubbish beside de front gate.

And why do you always feel the need to mention your ex
My face don't say angry, but just know that I'm vex.
And when we go out in public you always try and make a show
Hugging and kissing me, but when we get home
and I want sex you telling me no.
Imagine ladies, the mans eating my dinner and saying how it's nice
But then comparing me to his mother, and how she cook's her rice.

Please don't get it twisted… I'm not hating on you men
I'm just keeping it real for all the other women.

Men… why do you always rush us when we're getting dressed?
Our clothes, hair and make-up take time, we don't need to be stressed.
Then you take us out to your family events but leave us standing alone
So to keep the peace we smile and pretend we're
checking messages on our phone.
And why do we have to repeat ourselves
when you're not paying attention?
You're on your phone or watching TV when we're
supposed to be having a conversation.
We hear that men are from Mars and women are from Venus
And know there's a difference between us two
So men we just want you to Listen, Love us,
and give us the respect we're due.
We're not trying to change you.. honest
I just want you to be my man
Dress real smart, smell real good and do the best you can.
I'm not trying to tell you where to go, what to do or what to think
But I really think you'd look good in that shirt, especially if it was pink.

© 2016

SHE AIN'T HAPPY

It ain't about me myself and I
I will not be your alibi
I can only tell you what I know
Not about Sam, Michael or about Joe

This is about what's inside me
It's about my heart and soul
It's about how I feel and express
It's about all the emotions I control

Don't tell me that you know how I feel
You said you felt this way before
You can't compare me to your ex
Or the time she kicked you out the door

And, no, it's not the time of the month
And it's not my hormones
I really, really want you to tell me
Why you need to have 3 phones

Why you need to talk in secret
Or have conversations in another room
Why you leave the same time every evening
Saying "oh babes I'll be back soon"

You are hardly home for dinner
And now you're staying out all night
I don't need to be a genius
To know that something ain't quite right

There's no real communication
And you're always blaming me
But you need to try remembering
That we are your family

We're the ones that stand by you
And try our best not to complain
And even when you come with crap
We could leave, but we remain

I just want some appreciation
So stop disrespecting me
I'm the mother of your children
And your better half I'll always be

I'm supposed to be your best friend
And the one you whisper to
The day we stood in that church
You're the one that said "I do"

All I'm trying to say babes
Is that we need to communicate
We need to get to the root of the problem
Before it really becomes too late

I don't want to become a statistic
Or have children in a broken home
All I want to do is talk
So babes please……. put down that phone

© 2014

NO IDENTITY

I had short hair
On my face I had spots
I wasn't slim
And I wore polka dots.
I came from a different area
And I spoke with a twang
The other girls didn't like me
I wasn't apart of their gang.
My family didn't have much money
I cared for my sister like she was my own
I'd pick her up from nursery
Fed her and put her to bed when we got home.
I was only 13
And without a real friend
I should have been revising for exams
All this could have brought me to my end.
At home there was constant bickering
And at school they bullied me
I had no one to turn to
I felt I had no identity.
Some said I should report it
But the bullies were very smart
It always happened in private
I had no scars, just a broken heart.
I bleached my hair
Like they told me I should
I followed them around
But it did me no good.

I just couldn't fit in
I just didn't belong
At home or at school
I just didn't feel that strong.
I hated the bullies
But didn't know how to fight back
But then I found my voice
And used it as an attack.
I started rapping
And in that zone I was set free
I allowed no one to hold me down
That's when I found my identity.
I rapped about my life at school
And the bullies became my friends
I told them how they made me feel
And the bullying came to an end.

Keep your friends close, and your enemies closer.

© 2015

ELAINE GIBBONS

A GIRLS STORY

I met him at a party
And danced with him all night
He said that I should be his girl
And I told him that I might.

He was generous with his gifts
He was generous with his money
At first he was a perfect gentleman
And I always found him to be funny.

Six months later he began to change
He didn't want me to see my mates
He said he wanted me all to himself
And so he stopped taking me out on dates.

I'd met all his mates though
They'd all meet up in his front room
His phone was always ringing
He'd pop out but be back soon.

A year later he was still giving me gifts
Especially when I made him smile
He liked when I carried his packages
Even though it took a little while

To get to know that area
But then it didn't seem that hard
He'd drop me off in city centre
Then I'd get a cab back to his yard.

One of his friends said I was gorgeous
But I told him to leave me be
But my man begged me to go for a ride with him
But in his car he abused me.

After two years I had moved in with him
But now I feel such a fool
When the police raided his flat
They said I should have been in school.

They took all his packages
And all the money he had
They said I was a victim
I didn't think he treated me that bad.

At the time I was only 15
And knew he was twenty two
I really believed he loved me
But really didn't have a clue.

I had to move back home
Because he went to jail
I wrote him everyday
But he returned my mail.

I'm 19 now
And that's all in the past
It took along while to get over it
But I've finally moved on…at last.

© 2015

A BOYS STORY

My mom was never around
And my dad I never knew
My friends were my only family
When I didn't know what to do.

We were all in the same boat
My friends and I
They all looked out for me
Sometimes I'd be their alibi.

Sometimes the police would come by
And take them all away
But they'd be back on the street
Before the end of that day.

All of them were older than me
And always had expensive things
Jewellery, money and cars
I guess hustling dope was what that brings.

Fortune and fame
And respect in the hood
I really craved for some of that
And believed it was something good

And so I joined their crew
And not just for financial gain
I saw the behaviour and lifestyle
I didn't think what I did caused pain.

I didn't think of the impact on the community
I didn't think of it as organised crime
I was living beyond legitimate means
But didn't care about that at the time.

I was living large
And so kept chasing that paper
I was slinging rocks
If you got in my way, you'd meet your maker.

I found it so easy
And even better than cheese
I had my soldiers work it
So I could sit back with ease.

I thought I was invincible
Because I was flying high
The police said they had intelligence
That could link me to a drive by.

They arrested me on road
They took my phone, my car and keys
And when they raided my home
They took my twenty gees.

Easy come, easy go
The judge gave me 10 years
As I look back on my life
I'm sad but shed no tears.

So listen up people
Don't do what I've done
Don't make the same mistakes
Because your better than that my son.

© 2015

THE SYSTEM

Some don't want to sign on
But want some money
They don't have a job
But want to romance their honey.
I'm tired to talk
And tired to reason
Some take this thing for a joke
But everything has its season.
You can't expect money for nothing
You have to work for what you want
But some just aren't prepared to do it
You ask why, they shrug… I can't.
Some rush to make the easy money
But won't rush in the morning time
If they had a little common sense
They would walk and join the line.
Some say it's the government's way of holding them down
But how come, when you just have to sign your name?
Why don't you just take the government's money?
And then just play the game.
A little job search don't' hurt nobody
Just take it as a means to an end
Get out of it what you can
Then go set yourself a trend.
Go work for yourself
Or do that training course
Go get a job
But don't dare live with remorse.

Don't let time pass you by
Don't let the oppressors win
It's about making a positive change
And not having your C.V put in the bin.
You're worth more than that
You can make it if you try
Go get that job or business loan
And wave the system goodbye.
But first you have to know yourself
To make that positive change
You have to know where you're coming from
Then your life you can re-arrange.

© 2015

THEY KILL

Some say there's a lot of Guns on the street
But none did we ship or manufacture
They say nuff Guns on the street
And that's what the youths are running after

The Guns not nice
And the Guns not pretty
The Gun can mean the end
For a lot in Birmingham City

The Guns got no name
But can take a lot of lives
Brothers and sisters
And husbands and wives

It's heavy in the hand
And silent in the pocket
It carries a lot of weight
And some use it to profit

A second to pull the trigger
Can mean a life being taken away
And if it doesn't lead to death
Your conscience might kill you one day

You can't blame the trigger
And you can't blame the hand
There's no coming back from it
That's what I want you to understand

Possession of a firearm carries 10 to life
And that's just the prison time
Because once you've been released
You'll still be reminded of your crime

We need to live free from fear and violence
Too many of our youth are dying that way
If you're the one carrying a weapon
PLEASE, decide to put it down today

If you like to pack heat, strap up or carry
You need to take a stock
Because the judge won't joke to throw away the key
And behind you the prison gate lock

So please, I urge you again
To think before you make that mistake
Your life is worth so much more
But it's your choice and a chance you take.

© 2015

HE CHANGED

It all began
When he was running the street
He was living in darkness
But the money was sweet.

At first he was a soldier
And then became a Don
He worked night and day to prove himself
So it didn't take him that long.

Money, cars and women
He had his boys, he had his crew
These soldiers kept him going
Because they knew just what to do.

No work, no pay
They hustled to make that paper
Everyone wanted to get rich
But wanted it sooner not later.

The more he made
The more he lived in fear
A lot of jealous men were around
Who wanted his money and his gear.

He was always switching phones
And looking over his shoulder
He could trust no-one
He found out as he got older.

He lived a bad boy lifestyle
But got raided every now and then
But he wasn't ready to give up
So would just start all over again.

After some years he wanted out of the game
He wanted to live in peace
He wanted to see his kids grow up
And stop running from police.

It's not easy, it really isn't
God only knows how he tried
He tried to put it all behind him
Even when pressure was applied.

It took him a while, but he's free
He stands before you a better man
He stood up to his responsibilities
And now is a part of a positive plan.

So if you see him when you look in the mirror
You'll know these words are true
That life aint no life at all
So don't choose that game, live life for you.

© 2015

WHATS UP FAM?

You're not related by blood
But call them your family
You say they are down for you 24 seven
And for you that is the key
But when you got arrested
Did they put up yourbail?
And when you got your sentence
Did they come visit you in jail?
When your girl was suffering financially
Did they help to pay her bill?
When your son followed in your footsteps
What kind of words did they instill?
So now you're in jail
And your son is skipping school
Did your family encourage him?
Did they tell him that wasn't cool?
Did they look out for him
Just like you would?
Did they take on the responsibilities
Just like a family should
Don't get it twisted blood
Your family should be down like that
That's how they show love
They can't just do it with chat.

Inspired by David Skins

© 2016

DON'T DO IT

It's not just about the damage to your health
You get high, you miss work, don't go to school
You're on the street robbing people and shops
You hang around breaking every rule

The first high will never be achieved again
Your body becomes tolerant, you need more
More money to buy more drugs
So now you'll do anything just to score

You start to come down
More money and drugs you need
You sell possessions, commit more crime
And with family and friends you plead

You get paranoid and depressed
And may lose a lot of weight
You don't sleep and become moody
Your whole life's now in a bad state

Heroin, Cannabis, Crack and Cocaine
Those are some of the effects they cause
They will be mixed with other products to increase quality
You can never be sure what you're using, and that's the reality

You may roll up a twenty
And snort a line
You may even chase the dragon
And feel just fine

You might smoke some skunk
Or even some Crack
You might sniff some Cocaine
Or inject some smack

Legal highs are just as bad
Blue Cheese, Black Mamba and Spice
These all carry serious health risks
And the after effects are just not nice

Alcohol and Cigarettes
Are dangerous too
Cancer, Liver failure and Lung problems
Are some of the things that can happen to you

Don't try drugs out of curiosity
To have a good time or because you feel stressed
Not because your friends do it and you want to join in
Or even because you feel depressed

To recognise you have a problem
Puts you on the road to recovery
It takes a lot of courage and strength
But that's were you'll claim your Victory.

© 2015

NEW KIDS ON THE BLOCK

**The streets for the youth are cold
But for no other generation were they paved with gold.**

They look at you
And they look at me
We talk to them about life
But they talk of what they don't want to be.

Many don't want to do the 9 to 5
They say it just don't pay
They say they see us suffering
So in the Game they'd rather play.

Easy money's the attraction
They have no fear at all
Many of them are street wise
But without common sense nuff of them will fall.

Fall along the wayside
Because they're not willing to listen to reason
They know it all, so carry on
Not knowing that the consequence will come in due season.

They are a law unto themselves
As they carry their guns and knives
For argument over drugs or money
Some won't think to take other people's lives.

Overpopulated prisons
Or a sentence of more than five
Is not even a deterrent
As long as there alive.

They will terrorise our streets
And the community will live in fear
Why some chose to live this way
The answers not always clear.

There's a lot of professional help out here
But the youth don't know who to trust
We need to build a stronger partnership
Then they might let us in…. But only just.

Just enough to see what we're about
So the work needs to follow through
We need to do what we say we will
And not pass the buck from me to you.

They need a listening ear and friendly face
It helps if you come from the streets
And also if you can identify
And not just talk because your heart beats.

But I pledge to help those that I can
I'll encourage, I'll support and try change
The mindset of those that will listen
So that their lives, they can re-arrange.

Inspired by Craig Pinkney and others.

© 2015

YOU CAN SAY NO

Man's on the street
With nothing to do
With no where to go
Some ain't got a clue

They need to change their mindset
They need to get a grip
Because without direction
It's very easy to slip

Into the Gang culture
And carry Guns and Knives
And listen to others brag and boast
Of fast money and grand lifestyles

Don't follow the negative elders
Your perception of their lives ain't real
It's just a temporary illusion
But to live or die is such a big deal

Because it just don't last
Believe me it's true
But if you choose that road
It will have a real consequence for you

Because nuff mans in jail
With nothing to show
Nuff family and friends won't visit
And when their released they've no where to go

Always looking over your shoulder
Not being able to walk street at night
Having to hold a Mac 10 or pump action
Who wants to live like that, it ain't right

You have to walk in twos and threes
And carry a knife for your protection
That's your way of solving a problem
Or is it just in case of retaliation?

I know leaving a Gang ain't easy
But with support it can be done
You need some positive role models
You need to make better choices for yourself my son

There is nuff support out there
In the form of youth workers, mentors and more
You just need to believe you can change
And then walk into that open door.

© 2016

BLACK MALE

He's educated and smart
And often reasons from his heart
He has goals and ambition
And won't be held down by tradition.
This young man is a success
And so needs to be recognised
For the positive role model he is
He does not need to be criticised.
He'll work two jobs if he has to
Because he won't see his family without
Whether he lives with them or not
Because that's what he's all about.
He is a hard working young man
Who looks after his family
His partner and his children
Are his responsibility.
He's dark and handsome
He makes his friends and family proud
He leads by example
And doesn't follow the crowd.
Don't get me wrong
Other race of men do all this too
But I'm bigging up My Black Men
And giving them credit where it's due.

Inspired by Quintessential Rae.

© 2016

BACKLASH

It began in the 1980s
The Gangs were born out of poverty
They emerged from the Handsworth Riots
It started with petty crime and then robbery

It began in the 1980s
But escalated in two thousand and three
With the murder of two innocent girls
As they left a New Years day party

Crew members fell out over women and drugs
The postcodes were now divided
The community feared for their safety
But no protection for them was provided

The issues were respect, revenge and revenue
And violence was the order of the day
They both wanted to control the drug trade
But the postcodes were just 1 mile away

Like every other war
The police were involved
But due to witness intimidation
Most of the crimes just went unsolved

For 20 years they terrorised the City
Their notoriety can still be felt on the street
The community still fear for their safety
As the Police continue to walk on their beat

How foolish is this postcode war
As they sit together in jail
How can reputation mean more than life?
Some don't live to tell the tale

Educate yourselves young people
There has to be a better way
For you not to live your lives like this
You need Real Action in your lives today

Surround yourselves with positive people
It takes a man to stand his ground
Where are the elders you looked up to?
They are no where to be found

Except underground or in HMP
That life is not for you
There's always an alternative
In everything you do

But don't listen to me
Cos what do I know?
Except this little fact of life
"You can only reap the seeds you sow"

Inspired by Mr Holgate

© 2016

ELAINE GIBBONS

THESE DAYS

These days nobody can't talk to anybody missus
And the kids are even worse
You try and tell them right from wrong
And at you they want to curse.

Everybody think they're grown
Because a lot of them have their own key
A lot of children having children
But that's got nothing to do with me.

I expect manners and respect
Because it don't cost a thing
I won't accept bad behaviour
Because unhappiness it bring.

I couldn't talk to my parents any how
But the kids now want the last word
But when I was growing up
We had to be seen and not heard.

You couldn't whine you neck
Or put your hand on your kimbo
You had to stand straight
And shut up when an adult said so.

But these days nobody can't talk to anybody missus
You got to know how to send a text
You need to have email, instagram or twitter
And without Facebook a lot of people vex.

I don't have Iphone 6 or Galaxy
I just do my own thing
I don't have an Ipad or Macbook
I'm grateful if my Nokia ring

I can't keep up with all this technology
It's the young peoples thing that
I'm still happy to pick up my house phone
And after one hour stop chat.

I don't want BT, Talk Talk or Virgin
To send me a big bill at all
So I won't go over my minutes
Or make any unnecessary call.

I remember when the house phone had a lock
And our telly would take 50 pence
And when my dad was in the house
We couldn't play past the garden fence.

These days nobody can't talk to anybody missus
The kids are out from morning til night
They don't even tell you where they are
But when you ask they say they're alright.

But these days I give God thanks for his mercy
Cos I'm still here to tell this tale
I'm able to see the kids grow up
And decide whether to go to Harvard or Yale.

So people be blessed
And take care in your ways
I wish you all the best
And pray for peace in these days.

© 2015

DE PICKNEY DEM

Why de chile can't behave imself
Why de chile have to ansa back
Why im gwarn like im oldda dan me
An den wonda why im get a slap
But not arl de children gwarn so
Nuff a dem have mannars and respec
Nuff a dem cyan be doctors an laryers
Some a dem creative artists would mek
But me love de likkle pickney dem you see
Especially when dem dress fi go a school
Wid dem fade, pig tails an curly hair
I jus hope dem remember de rule
Not to speak unless spoken to
An not to ansa back
Not to get involve in big people convasation
Oddawise dem will get a slap.
De bible seh don't spare de rod and spwile de chile
Nuff a dem need discipline yes
I not condoning violence
Cos nuff parents try dem bess.
So children, obey you parents
And parents listen dem too
Because unnu neva too ole fi learn
In anyting unnu do.
But seriously, me love de likkle pickney dem
Especially when dem grow big and fine
And dem get dem cerfiticket and degree
But den you cyan only tark to dem pon line.

Oh come everyting is about computer?
Three gig, four G an EE
Me don't undastan it at arl
Me grandson do…an im only three
Well now dem arl grow big and buy ouse
Some of dem apartments ar two
Dem ave good job and big wages
An me really proud of dem fi true.
But me arlways tell dem dis you know
Mannars and respec will get you far
Qualifications cyan give you dat
Even wen you tun big supastar.
So young people I wish unna arl de bess
In everyting unnu do
Sometimes I wish I was young again
Den again…..me is only 22

© 2015

WOMEN

We're more than just female
Or that girl for that boy
We're more than just partners
And certainly nobody's toy
We're more than just mothers
Waiting at the school gate
We're more than patient
When the housekeeping is late.
We're more than just a body in the kitchen
Or a playmate in bed
We're more than just a help mate
Or didn't you hear what I just said.
We're more than a shoulder to cry on
When things go wrong
We're more than able to leave
If we feel we don't belong.
We're more than knitting jumpers
Or that needle and thread
We're more than just giving birth
Or carrying baskets on our head.

We're kind and loving
More than independent and strong
We can fight our battles
And of cause we're never wrong.
We're not all bossy
Crazy, clingy or cold
Intense or high maintenance
But grow graceful when old.

ELAINE GIBBONS

We're not all angry or feisty
Hormonal or brash
We're not all frivolous spenders
Who just buy clothes with our cash.

We walk with elegance
And carry ourselves with grace
We're beautifully and wonderfully made
And that's the thrill of the chase.
We're fashionable, spiritual
And funny as well
We're happy and intelligent
And sexy no hell.
We're fantastic and fabulous
We're gorgeous and great
We're wonderful, phenomenal
Yes I'm just giving it to you straight.

We're Wise and Wonderful Women
One of a special kind
Made by Gods fair hands
And a better species you'll never find.
So embrace us, love us
And let us live
In an equal and peaceful society
Because we have so much more to give.

© 2016

REMEMBER WHEN

I remember when
You either eat lunch at school or you go home
But nowadays de pickney dem
Outside de chip shop pon dem phone.

I remember when
Kids would only fight with mouth and fists
But today many use knives
As if is only dem fe exis

I remember when we had no worries
There was no Insta, Facebook or tweets
But no pickney a get bully pon line
And de youths dem a run de streets.

De whole community is now fearful
Of violence, scams and bank fraud
Of being bullied, abused and being killed
Dese tings even happen when you go abroad.

I remember when it was a time of peace
And you would tark to you neighbour across de garden fence
But no everybody fence 6 foot high
As if crossing de border would have a consequence.

As kids we love playin in de garden
Come wind, rain or shine
Dese days kids not interested inna dat
Cos dem nar leave dem phone, Ipad ar PlayStation behine

I remember when it was dinna time
And de whole family would all eat de same
But nowadays one pickney no eat dis and de adda no eat dat
I just don't know who to blame.

When my parants use to tark
I couldn't seh no, kiss teet or ansa back
But nowadays pickney wha argue, stamp foot, slam door
Lard, dem really a get slack.

We had to respeck we elders
Sunday school was not a choice
But dem was de good ole days
We wouldn't dare mek de same mistake twice.

I no tings and times change
And not evryting cyan stay de same
But when it comes to respeck an mannas
I believe dats sumting evry kid should claim.

I want dese kids to have some good ole days
An nuff positive tings to remember
So me and de nex generation
Gonna work to have better days together.

So let's try and remember
To give thanks in de marning and an at night
Cos tomorrow no promise to nun a we
So todeh, mek we try live right.

ME DEAR CHILE

Imagine, my daughter pass out arl har exam dem
And have nuff certificate pon me warl
She fine man, get married and shoudda happy
But turn up a me house a barl.

So of cause me arsk har what wrong
When we chile dun tark me nearly dead
After she tell me how she cum home
And fine har husband an anadda woman in bed.

What more me could a do but hush me chile
Even thou she turn 50 years
Me neva have dis problem wid har fardda
But dem ya man nowadays…..

Dem have one and a look anadda
I don't care if de grass greener pon de adda side
Nurture what you got an it will grow
An stop play seek and hide.

Him tell har seh it was a mistake
Him seh de woman drug him tea
Him neva no wha him did a do
Me arsk har what kine a fool him be.

My chile seh she wha go cuss de woman
Me tell har seh if she do dat, she wrong
Is har husband she fe cuss
And den she fe ole har head and be strong.

Me tell har seh me neva raise no fool
But if she love him she cyan forgive
Because nobody no perfek, marriage tek work
An is fe har own life fe live.

So my daughta decide to forgive him
And dem been going on now five years
Dem boat seem in love and happy
Tank God me never affe shed no tears.

because me no nuff woman would a tell har fe leff him
But dem words I would neva seh
Cos when dem didda seh dem vows
Ah no me and dem did deh.

So mek we leave people business alone
Try live in peace, and ten to we own
Cos in life we fe neva seh neva
Judge others, complain ar moan.

No dig no ditch fe nobody
And try not to have no badmine
Just try fine you place in life
And let love surround you all the time.

SOME BLACK HISTORY

Is not jus about Octoba
It began wid me parents an fiddem history
So mek me begin wid dem
And fiddem story.

De two a dem cum from Jamaica
At a time when tings did really rough
But dem mek demself content and happy
Even wen de going did get tough.

Dem neva come wid much money
Just a couple clothes, 2 shoes and 1 hat
But dem have love, mannas and respeck fe each adda
You couldn't arsk fe more dan dat.

Me madda use to work a day
And me fardda work a night
Sometimes five a we share one bed
We had no choice, but it was alright.

Back den it was to home
To church and always to school
We had to do as we was told
Because dat was de golden rule.

We couldn't answer back
Ar tark we attitude
We had to be seen and not heard
Cos there would be hell to pay if you was rude.

Me madda had a twin tub
An she teach me fe wash by han
But me smarl clothes couldn't go in de machine
Not like nowadays when everything cyan.

Satdeh daytime de hardwork would begin
That was de time to cook, iron and clean
Den we'd watch wrestling wid big daddy and giant haystacks
After dinner we'd eat jelly and ice-cream.

Mom teach me how fe scrub de dutch pot
Scarl milk and wash inna beardin pan
We swinge de chicken on Frideh
And if me use de smarl spoon de ice-cream will lars long.

We use to clock 50pence inna de tv
But couldn't use de phone cos it de lock
Me use to pay de pop man pon Satdeh
And watch Crossroads after 6 O'Clock.

We had to go straight home from school
And mek sure seh me clothes fix wen me reach de front door
And when me madda give me 20pence pocket money
Me couldn't dare arsk har fe more.

Cos me neva give me madda money fe puddung
Every penny she get buy milk and bread
An if me and me siblings farm fool and mek noise
Me fardda would sen us early to bed.

Me an me broddas and sistas
Share nuff love and larfta
So no me a share my history
Wid my son and daughta.

I'm a proud madda and granmadda
Wid so much more to share
I am black History
I can neva be erased, so try if you dare.

THE YOUTH OF TODAY 2019

The youth of today are a struggle
They're shooting, stabbing, many die
This is a way of life for some
We need to find the reasons why.

Why many fathers are missing
Why many mothers just can't cope
Why many children are left to fend for themselves
And why some turn to alcohol or dope.

So what's the answer I hear you ask?
I don't presume to have them all
But I know we have a responsibility
To stop others from the same downfall.

So let's talk about why some join gangs
Some say they get protection from others
They have no positive role models
So the gang become their sisters and brothers.

They say they want to be accepted
And to feel a part of a family
They join to get respect
And to be supported emotionally.

Others join for a sense of identity
And because they think it's cool
Other family members may be affiliated
So they don't want to be an outcast, or look like a fool.

So now it's about peer pressure
And for some it's financial gain
They're not able to see their future
To them life is one big game.

Many live for today with no hope for tomorrow
Many suffer with mental health
Whilst still inflicting pain and sorrow.

We know the youth are not all like this
But we are losing them at an alarming rate
We must rain them all back in
Because for many others it may be too late.

We've lost too many to the gangs
And lost many to the drugs men
We've lost too many to violence
It needs to stop now…..if not then when?

We need to help them find alternatives
So they're not shaped by what they see on the streets
Because they're not theirs…the streets
But are all our heart beats.

We need to be open and talk to the youth
And listen without interrupting
We need to ask them what we can do to help
And that is just the beginning.

So get involved in your child's life
Try and understand things from their point of view
Because we were all young once
This is just a simple message from me, to you.

THIS WAS HER REALITY

Hell on earth was how she described her life
She felt she just couldn't cope
Her husband had left and taken the kids
She was living without a hope.

She was no longer the breadwinner
And felt she could no longer provide
Security for her family
All she was left with was her pride.

In her flat she'd cook a meal for one
In front of the TV she'd sit alone
She felt friends and family had disserted her
As no one would call her on her phone.

She had too much time to sit and think
Her thoughts became dark and deep
Surrounding all the mistakes she'd made
And the promises she didn't keep.

She missed work and wouldn't venture out
She said she just couldn't go
The shame of having nothing at all
Left her feeling very low.

She was diagnosed with Anxiety and Depression
That's what all the Doctors had said
She struggled on a daily basis
Just to get out of her bed.

She said my head was full of so much noise
And my heart with so much pain
I'm just sick and tired of crying
Over and over and over again.

She was sick of people telling her to get over it
To be positive and to be strong
She lost everything and felt so low
She was constantly asking, how long.

She said she had always looked after her family
And always worked from 9 to 5
But didn't feel anyone understood her
Or that she was battling to stay alive.

She went on to say, each day was a chore
She just felt sad and couldn't sleep
She overate to comfort herself
Then sat and cried when her feelings ran deep.

She felt tired and hopeless
She felt guilty and ashamed
To the outside world she had everything
But these feelings still remained.

Depression is a real illness
So let others know that you care
Accept people without judgement
Because for others life can really seem unfair.

The message I'm trying to send you
Is to be good and kind to others
Don't see people in need and do nothing
Because life is precious, and that's what matters.

HOW TO CONTACT THE AUTHOR

Contact Elaine Gibbons

mzsaintmartin@aol.com
www.facebook.com/elaine.gibbons

Feel free to contact me for book orders or readings at events. I also frame poems and poster size to A3.

My previous books, A Poets Dream and Live a little love a lot can be found on Amazon.

May I take this opportunity to thank you again for your support.

FUTURE EVENTS – 29th July 2016 - Birmingham Caribbean Festival
                               20th August 2016 – The MAC Birmingham

Please contact me for further information.

www.ingramcontent.com/pod-product-compliance
Lightning Source LLC
Chambersburg PA
CBHW030909080526
44589CB00010B/220